Models for Writing

Pupil's Book 5

Chris Buckton
Anne Sanderson

Series editor: Leonie Bennett

   GINN

Symbols

 Group/individual work.

PCM A photocopy master is available to support differentiation.

Differentiation symbols.

1 Easy to complete.

2 All pupils complete activity. Activities are supported by a PCM for extra help.

3 More difficult activities.

Author Team: Chris Buckton
                Anne Sanderson
Series Editor: Leonie Bennett

Ginn
Linacre House, Jordan Hill, Oxford, OX2 8DP
a division of Reed Educational and Professional Publishing Ltd
www.ginn.co.uk

Ginn is a registered trademark of Reed Educational and Professional Publishing Ltd

ISBN 0602 296889

04 03 02 01 00
10 9 8 7 6 5 4 3 2

Designed and produced by Gecko Ltd, Bicester, Oxon
Cover design by Gecko Ltd, Bicester, Oxon
Printed in Spain by Edelvives

Contents

RECOUNT
Chilham Castle

We went to Chilham Castle on October 19th as part of our project on the Middle Ages. Chilham Castle is in Kent so we had to go by train.

First of all we met at Victoria Station. Manny wasn't
5 there. We had to bring packed lunch. Mine was chicken sandwiches. We were in the train for an hour.

At last we got off the train and walked up a hill. It was beautiful. We walked for a long time, then a lady appeared dressed in medieval clothes. She had a head dress with a
10 veil which was embroidered with pearls. Her clothes were embroidered too because she was a rich lady. She showed us her husband called the Knight of the Black Gauntlet. Inside his helmet his voice sounded all muffled. Then he took his helmet off and said that we were the only group
15 who didn't say 'Cor ain't he old!'

Next he showed us his weapons, which were two swords, and a battle axe. The thought of using them made me shake. Then we found out that jousting meant the same as training, and that they used a dummy knight called a
20 quintain. He got on his horse and charged at the quintain.

Then the lady put out some foam heads for him to try and spear. In medieval times they would have been real heads because they wanted to show the enemy how great they were. I think it was savage.

25 I learned quite a lot about knights and the Middle Ages that day.

by Claire, age 9

opening – sets the scene

past tense

varied connectives

records events as they happened

closing statement

Reading

1. Write down three things that you think Claire does well in writing her recount.

2. Write down two things that you think she could improve.

3. Imagine that you are Claire. Write a letter to a friend about the trip to Chilham.

Writing

PCM 2

1. Write the first draft of a recount for an audience that you don't know. You can either finish the draft begun in shared writing, or use your homework notes.

2. Swap your writing with someone else. Check whether it includes all the recount features. Give it a point for each feature.

REMEMBER

Make sure you have used varied connectives.

Extended Writing

Revise your first draft. Make any improvements then check spellings and punctuation.

Reading Logs

Peter's List

Everything I read yesterday

clock (does this count?)
cereal packet
TV Times
junk mail about free mag
postcard from Ben
road signs
poster about concert

ad about choc
sweet shop labels on desperate choc hunt
class notices
hymn words in assembly
music notes (does this count?)
swimming cert – me = genius!
blackboard notes in science
literacy hour stuff inc dictionary
maths book
computer screen
Point Horror – Aargh!!!!!
TV
Forget the rest.

abbreviations

NB work out how much time spent reading?

Beth's Reading Log

Z for Zachariah by Robert O'Brien

14 May – 1st chapter seems to be a bit weird sometimes I get the gist of the story and then think what's happening?! Only thing I understand so far is that a girl and her family are living somewhere and every one is dead around them! Wow!

16 May – Reading on now I know that the girl's family has gone away and she's trying to make the house look not lived in! What's going on?

17 May – Her family hasn't come back so she is making preparations for surviving on her own forever and I'm only on page 17 and I'm in a complete muddle! Some of it gives me the creeps.

22 May – This girl who has all this happen to her seems to take everything in her stride does she have any feelings?

23 May – Think now I'm starting to get the idea of what is going on, actually it is getting quite good there is now a man there she has been watching him for days and the dog has come back so I'm just waiting to see what happens next. Still think that the girl has no feelings except for her tingle of excitement when she first heard the man's voice!

26 May – She is living in a cave now and watching every move he makes I wish she would speak to him let him know she's there. But I do understand her reasons but she must speak to him sooner or later I hope so any-way.

work out the story as you go

sorting out feelings

your feelings about the story

Reading

❶ Make your own list of everything you read yesterday. Did you and Peter read any of the same things?

❷ a What does Beth feel about the book at first?

   b What does she feel about the girl?

   c What does she think might happen next?

   d How does she change her mind about the book as she goes on reading?

Writing

❶ Choose what you want to write about in your reading log. It should be something you have read recently.

❷ Write the date in your reading log.

PCM
4

❸ Start writing! Don't worry about spelling or handwriting. Just get your ideas down.

REMEMBER

Write about something you have read that matters to you.

A reading log is a way of sorting out your ideas and feelings.

A reading log is <u>not</u> a review.

Extended Writing

Continue writing in your log.

FICTION

The Dark Streets of Kimball's Green

Joan Aiken

begins with speech →

'Em! You, Em! Where has that dratted child got to? Em! Wait till I lay hold of you. I won't half tan you!'

Mrs Bella Vaughan looked furiously up and down the short street. She was a stocky woman, with short, thick, straight
5 grey hair, parted on one side and clamped back by a grip; a cigarette always dangled from one corner of her mouth and, as soon as it dwindled down, another grew there. 'Em! Where have you got to?' she yelled again.

'Here I am, Mrs Vaughan!' Emmeline dashed anxiously ←
10 round the corner.

uses adverbs

→ 'Took long enough about it! The Welfare Lady's here, wants to know how you're getting on. Here, let's tidy you up.'

Mrs Vaughan pulled a comb and a handkerchief out of her tight-stretched apron pocket, dragged the comb sharply ←
15 through Emmeline's hair, damped the handkerchief with spit and scrubbed it over Emmeline's flinching face.

new paragraph when someone speaks

'Hullo, Emmeline. Been out playing?' said the Welfare Lady, indoors. 'That's right. Fresh air's the best thing for them, isn't it, Mrs Vaughan?'

20 'She's always out,' grunted Mrs Vaughan. 'Morning, noon and night. I don't hold with kids frowsting about indoors. Not much traffic round here.'

'Well, Emmeline, how are you getting on? Settling down with Mrs Vaughan, quite happy are you?'

25 Emmeline looked at her feet and muttered something. She was thin and small for her age, dark-haired and pale-cheeked.

'She's a mopey kid,' Mrs Vaughan pronounced. 'Always want to be reading, if I didn't tell her to run out of doors.'

30 'Fond of reading, are you?' the Welfare Lady said kindly. 'And what do you read, then?'

'Books,' muttered Emmeline. The Welfare Lady's glance strayed to the huge, untidy pile of magazines on the telly.

'Kid'll read anything she could lay hands on, if I let her,' 35 Mrs Vaughan said. 'I don't know though. What good does reading do you? None that I know of.'

uses
adverbs

10

Reading

PCM 5

1 Find words and phrases from the text to describe Mrs Vaughan and Emmeline.

2 a How do you think Emmeline feels about Mrs Vaughan?

b What do you think Emmeline muttered to herself when the Welfare Lady asked, 'How are you getting on?'.

3 How do you think Mrs Vaughan would treat Emmeline when they were alone together? Make notes for what she might say to Emmeline.

Writing

PCM 7

What might Emmeline have done and felt while she was shut out of the house? Write the next paragraph of the story.

REMEMBER

Use adjectives and adverbs to describe how people speak.

Think about how each character feels.

How does each character behave?

Extended Writing

Write a description of what happens next. What happens when Mrs Vaughan comes back?

11

WORD PLAY

Concrete Poems

The Witch's Cat

ear ear

whiskers whiskers whiskers whiskers whiskers whiskers

The green beady eyes of the witch's cat, stare at me, glare at me. Its crow- black fur glistened with fury. Its back arched up and tail swung round. It whipped up its head and....h..ow..led. Its screech echoed around, nearly brought the house down. Then ... it turned and looked at me with an evil glare, with a horrible stare; Then it seemed to change, and, with needle-sharp teeth, as white as stars, it turned and trotted, proudly ... a ... w ... a ... y !

Jane Age 10

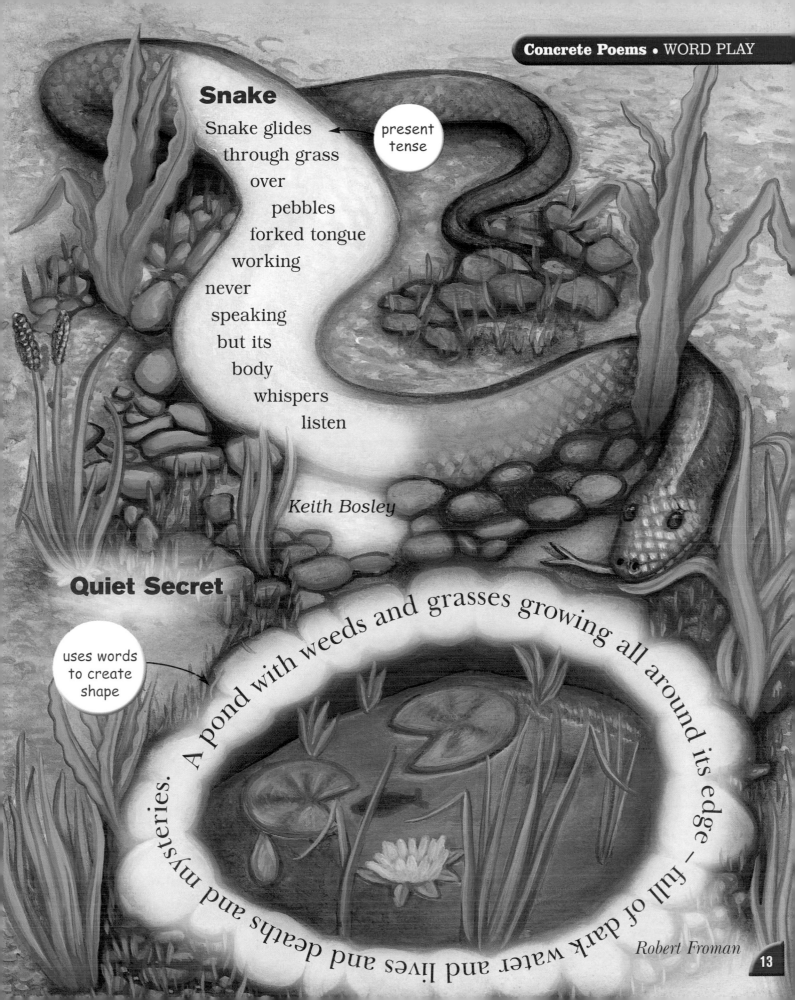

Snake

Snake glides
through grass
over
   pebbles
forked tongue
working
never
speaking
but its
body
whispers
   listen

present
tense

Keith Bosley

Quiet Secret

uses words
to create
shape

A pond with weeds and grasses growing all around its edge — full of dark water and lives and deaths and mysteries.

Robert Froman

Reading

1 Finish this sentence:

The poem I like most is ....

because ....

2 Look at the poems '**Witch's Cat**', '**Snake**' and '**Quiet Secret**'. With a partner decide:

- which words or groups of words do you like best?
- how do the words make you feel?

Writing

Working in pairs, do one of these.

1 Use **sheet 8** to write your own snail shape poem. You could use the ideas from shared writing as well as thinking of your own words.

OR

2 Write a concrete poem on the subject of your choice. Draw a feint outline of the shape before you start writing.

REMEMBER

Use the layout of the words to create a shape.

Use words which build up a picture or which add description.

Extended Writing

Finish your concrete poem and write it out neatly for display or to be included in a class book.

CHARACTER

The Angel of Nitshill Road

Anne Fine

Out in the corridor, Barry Hunter pushed his way over to
Celeste. You could tell from the look on his face that he
was going to pay her out for trying to tell on him.

Calmly, Celeste waited till he was two feet away, then
5 opened her mouth and screamed. Everyone stopped
shoving towards the two cloakrooms and turned to stare.
No one had ever heard anything like it. You'd think a
police car had switched on its siren inside a biscuit tin.
The noise was prodigious.

10   Barry Hunter backed off, fast.

As promptly as she'd turned the
scream on, Celeste turned it off again.

'You'll catch it if Mrs Brown heard
that,' Barry Hunter jeered.

15 'You'll catch it, too,' warned Celeste. 'I'll
tell her all the things you did to Mark.'

Just as she said his name, Mark stumbled
out of the classroom, last as usual, and
tripped over one of his own feet.

20   Barry Hunter snorted with amusement.

'I don't know why you keep sticking up
for him,' he said scornfully to Celeste.
'He's *weird.*'

Mark's face went scarlet. 'I'm not weird!'

25 'Well, you're not *normal*, are you?'
taunted Barry. He poked Mark in the chest
and peered closely at his face through the
thick bottle glasses, as if he were looking
at some insect though a microscope. 'No.
30 You couldn't say you were *normal.*'

new line
for each
person
speaking

speech
in speech
marks

adverbs
and verbs
describe how
characters
speak

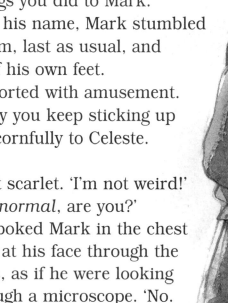

Suddenly Celeste was there, between the two of them.

'And you *are*, are you?' she demanded. She turned to everyone in the corridor – not just the people from their own class, but everyone else who was shuffling into the cloakrooms.

'Who wants to be *normal*, if normal's like Barry Hunter? Barry Hunter's a bully! He's spiteful and horrid! He steals and hides things! He's a slyboots and his only real pleasure comes from making the people round him unhappy! So who wants to be *normal*?'

She gazed round.

'Come on! Speak up! Say if you want to be *normal*!'

The dead silence in the corridor spread to the cloakrooms on either side. Everyone was watching Barry Hunter and Celeste. But no one said a word.

vivid character description

Reading

1 Scan lines 4–30 and complete each sentence with an adverb.

a
Celeste waited ....

b
Barry Hunter backed off ....

c
Barry peered .... at Mark.

2 a What sort of person is Celeste?

b What sort of person is Barry?

3 Read lines 36–40. Write down the words which describe Barry. Think of some more of your own then fill in the character web for Barry on **sheet 9**.

Writing

1 Continue writing the dialogue you began in shared writing. Think of a good ending for the argument.

2 Add another character to the scene. Write some dialogue for your new character. Think of a good ending for the scene.

REMEMBER

Make the speech fit the character.

Use adverbs to describe **how** *people speak.*

Rules for dialogue:

speech marks

capital letters

commas

new line for new speaker

Extended Writing

Develop your characters further by writing the opening to a different story about them. You could continue the story in future weeks.

PLAYSCRIPT

Working Children

Wes Magee

Scene 1

Place: *a busy street*
Time: *Victorian times (about 150 years ago)*

People pass by along the street. Harry and Beth, two hungry orphans, try to attract their attention.

 adverbs explain how lines should be spoken

HARRY:	Spare a farthing! Give us a farthing!
BETH:	*(miserably)* Anything for a starving girl? A crust of bread?
HARRY:	Spare a farthing, Guv? Give us a farthing!
BETH:	Anything for a hungry girl, lady? Anything?
HARRY:	Spare a farthing! Give us a farthing?
BETH:	Anything for a starving girl? A crust of bread?
1ST LADY:	What disgusting urchins.
2ND LADY:	They're everywhere. The town's full of brats, begging.
1ST LADY:	*(pointing)* Just look at those children! Just look at their clothes!
2ND LADY:	Call those clothes? Nothing but rags, filthy rags.
1ST LADY:	And their feet are bare. And what horrible feet. Ugh!
2ND LADY:	Don't go near them. You'll catch a disease. Come on.

(They pass by.)

HARRY: Spare a farthing!

BETH: Got a crust of bread? Just a crust of stale bread?

HARRY: Give us a farthing, Guv?

(A grim-looking man stops and then walks slowly round the children as if inspecting them.)

stage directions

SCRAGSCUTT: And who are you two, eh? What's with all this shouting?

HARRY: We're begging, sir. We're hungry. This is my young sister, Beth, and she's –

BETH: Starving!

SCRAGSCUTT: Hungry are you? Starving, eh? And what are your parents doing about it? Why aren't they looking after you, eh?

HARRY: Our parents are dead, sir. We're orphans.

SCRAGSCUTT: Orphans … well now, isn't that just one big surprise. Orphans, eh? And you've got no food.

HARRY: That's right, sir.

SCRAGSCUTT: And you've got no money.

BETH: That's right, sir.

SCRAGSCUTT: Well, maybe I can help you. Have you … er … ever worked, eh?

HARRY: Worked? No, sir. We're too young.

SCRAGSCUTT: Oh, you're never too young, lad. Maybe I can teach you to work. Yes, I'm sure you'd like to earn some money … and to have a good dinner, wouldn't you?

HARRY: Oh yes, sir.

SCRAGSCUTT: And how old are you?

HARRY: I'm nine –

BETH: And I'm eight.

SCRAGSCUTT: Just right! Just the ticket! Look, you two youngsters follow me and I'll … er … find a place for you to stay. And I'll … er … find you a job of work. Heh, heh! You'll soon learn how to work hard! You call me Scragscutt. That's all you need to know. Just follow me …

(He exits, followed by Harry and Beth.)

Reading

1. In groups, work through the script on **sheet 10**. Mark it to show:
   - what the characters are like
   - who will read each part
   - how the lines will be spoken.

2. Write stage directions. For example, add words to describe the actions and expressions of the children and Scraggscutt.

3. Read the script together. Remember, the way you read tells the audience about the personalities and feelings of the characters.

4. Continue marking up the rest of the scene on **sheet 11**.

Writing

1. Make notes to help you turn the story on **sheet 12** into a playscript.
   Who is speaking? What do they say? How do they speak?

2. Start to write the story out as a playscript. Use stage directions to show how the lines should be read.

PCM
13

REMEMBER

Stage directions explain what is happening, and how the lines should be spoken. Put them in brackets and italics, e.g.

BETH: *(whispering)* It looks a bit cold down there.

Use punctuation (! ? , .) to help show how lines should be spoken.

Extended Writing

Continue writing your playscript. Try reading it aloud with your group. How could you improve it?

METAPHOR

People Poems

My Headteacher

He's a bouncy chair,
He's a bright red door always open, ← paints a vivid picture
He's a barking, sudden dog,
A falcon flying to the sun,
The smell of a poppy,
adjectives → The sound of singing,
A sparkling morning with a sharp shower,
A fizzy drink,
A magician.

Adam, age 8

Reading

1 Using the subjects below, write down two more metaphors that fit Adam's headteacher:

- a food
- a time of year.

2 Finish these sentences:

> The headteacher is like a fizzy drink because ...
> He is like a barking dog because ...

Writing

PCM 15

1 Decide who you are going to write about. You could make up new things to compare your person with.

2 Write your own 'people poem'.

3 Read the first draft to your partner:

- Ask them to describe the sort of person they imagine your character to be.
- Are they right?
- Discuss ways you could improve the poem.

REMEMBER

Choose somebody you feel strongly about.

Use adjectives to make the connection clear.

Use metaphors.

Make each picture as vivid as you can.

Extended Writing

1 Revise your poems and make a neat copy for a class collection.

2 Choose one person to write a 'people poem' about.

STORY OPENINGS

Grab the Reader

exciting dialogue

From **Vera Pratt and the Bishop's False Teeth** *by Brough Girling*

'I KNOW EXACTLY WHAT YOU ARE DOING,' shouted the Bishop. 'YOU'RE PINCHING MY PETROL!'

'No, I ain't!' said his new chauffeur. 'We was just checking to see that the car was OK!'

'That is a lie!' said the Bishop: and he was right.

He had just got up, and had been having a nice little walk in the grounds of his Palace before breakfast, when he had come round the corner of his garage and seen something that, if he had had any hair, would have made it stand on end. As it was, his mouth had fallen open in horror.

His car was half-way out his garage, and behind it was a very large and dilapidated van with the words

ABC GARAGE

– petrol and repairs

gets into the action

on the side of it.

From **The Eighteenth Emergency** *by Betsy Byars*

builds
scene

The pigeons flew out of the alley in one long swoop and settled on the awning of the grocery store. A dog ran out of the alley with a torn Cracker Jack box in his mouth. Then came the boy.

catches
our
interest

The boy was running hard and fast. He stopped at the sidewalk, looked both ways, saw that the street was deserted and kept going. The dog caught the boy's fear, and he started running with him.

introduces characters

starts with a mystery

From **The Water Horse** *by Dick King-Smith*

It was Kirstie who found it. It was lying just above the high tide mark, a squarish package-shaped object, the colour of seaweed, with a long tendril sticking out from each of its four corners.

It was exactly the shape, in fact, of the 'mermaids' purses, the little horny egg capsules of the dogfish, that were commonly washed up on the beach. But this one was the size of a large biscuit tin.

'Look what I've found!' shouted Kirstie. 'Quick, come and look!'

Reading

1 Complete **sheet 16**.

2 Which opening grabs your interest most? Write a sentence to say why.

Writing

PCM 18

1 In pairs, look at the last two sentences from **The Water Horse** (beginning '*Look what I've found…*'). Use them to begin a story of your own. Make notes about the setting, characters and what might happen, then write the rest of the opening paragraph.

2 Working on your own, start planning the rest of your story.

REMEMBER

Openings

grab the reader

can introduce characters and setting

Person

be careful not to slip from third person (he/she) into first person (I)

Extended Writing

1 Finish planning your story. Make sure you include a lot of detail but keep it in note form.

2 Use your plan as a basis for writing a story.

How to make Paper Planes
The KH01 Prototype

numbered steps

You will need:

a sheet of paper
21cm × 29.5 cm (A4)

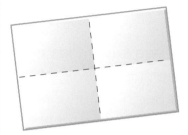

1

Fold a piece of paper down the middle. Unfold it. Fold it down the middle in the other direction. These folds are your guidelines.

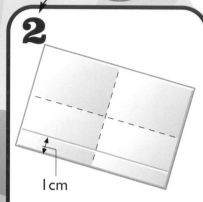

2

1cm

Score a line 1cm from the long edge. Then fold the paper up along this line.

3

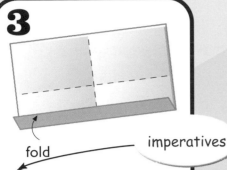

fold — *imperatives*

Fold the paper again and again until your folded edge reaches the middle guide line.

4

press and pull

The last fold has to be really tight, so press your ruler down hard on the paper and run it along the edge.

5

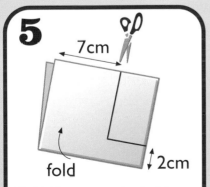

7cm

fold

2cm

Fold the paper in half with the folded paper on the inside. Draw and cut out the aeroplane shape as shown.

TROUBLESHOOTING

If it Stalls

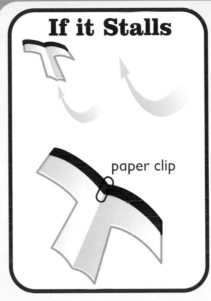

paper clip

Your plane may stall. It stalls because its nose is not heavy enough. Try putting a paper clip on its front. Or try putting a bit of tape along the folded edge.

If it Dives

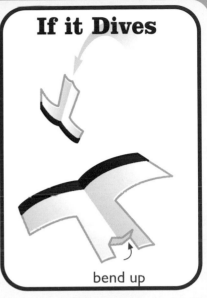

bend up

Your plane may dive to the ground if the nose is too heavy. Or maybe the tail is not working properly. Make a small cut each side of the tail and bend the paper up.

HANDY TIPS

FOLDING THE PAPER IN HALF

hold edges together with fingers

Your paper folds must be really accurate. The best way is to hold the edges together with your fingers while you smooth the fold down with your thumbs.

SCORING

diagrams help

Lay the paper on something hard and flat. Put your ruler along the line you want to score. Rule a line with a ball point pen. Press the pen down hard all the time.

Reading

1 Follow the instructions to make the paper plane. Compare your plane with a partner's plane.

2 Were the instructions easy to follow?

Writing

Work with a partner.

1 Make a paper dart, hat, boat or fortune teller, then unfold it. Go over the steps needed to make it.

2 Write Step 1. Sketch a diagram.

3 Roughly draft the next instruction and sketch a diagram.

4 Continue drafting the rest of the instructions, sketching a diagram for each step.

5 Now make the object using your instructions. Are they clear? Have you missed anything out?

REMEMBER

Use numbered steps.

Use imperative verbs.

Draw clear diagrams.

PCM 20

Extended Writing

Revise your instructions and make a neat copy. Swap your instructions with another pair and evaluate their work. Try out your instructions with younger pupils if you can.

PERSONAL EXPERIENCE

An Interview with Michael Morpurgo

'How do you get your ideas?'

'They come from the world around me. I live a very full life and keep my eyes and ears open. That's the first requirement, being aware of what's going on.'

'Do you write every day?'

'I make notes each day when I get home. I scribble down a line or two – a little tale, or something someone said, maybe funny, or desperately sad. Later on, sometimes twenty years later, that idea will re-emerge and connect to another idea and that's when the magic happens. Once I've got the embryo of the story, I warm the egg, then I'm ready to write. I go somewhere quiet and I write fast for long hours in terribly small handwriting, and keep at it, keep it flowing.'

'Do you have favourite places you write about?'

'Places I can really see, that I know well, like the Scilly Isles, and Devon.'

'Do you plan what's going to happen right the way through the story?'

'When I first started I thought you had to know right through to the end, but once I've got the idea I let it find its own way. The best things I've written have been when the characters take over, then the magic happens.'

'Do you revise your work as you go along or at the end of the first draft?'

'I make lots of changes as I go along. I read it aloud, or tape it and play the tape back to myself, to hear the rhythm, so it comes alive. After a chapter or so I rework the whole thing.'

revise
and edit

'Do you show anyone your work when you're in the middle of it?'

'Generally my wife. She's very good for spotting bits which don't seem real, or bits that are too flowery.'

'Could you explain how all the ideas for The Butterfly Lion came together?'

'There were a few things. I was told a story about a young man who went to the First World War and got wounded. While he was recovering in a little French village, he heard some shooting. It turned out to be a circus owner shooting his animals because there was no food for them. The true story is that the soldier saved an old lion, and walked back to his regiment with it. It was brought back to England and given to a zoo.

'I still couldn't make any headway with the story because I didn't know anything about lions. But the next thing was a chance meeting in a lift with someone who did know about lions.

'And then one day I heard a homesick child crying. It triggered a memory of a time when I was at school and homesick and I ran away. All these things came together to make the story.'

personal experience

'What advice would you give to young writers?'

'Write about what you know about and care about. Go out and see things and look at things.'

Reading

PCM
21

1 Choose one story you have written recently.

   a Where did your ideas come from?

   b How did you plan it?

   c How did you revise it?

   d Who did you show it to?

2 Think of things from your own experience that might be useful in a story. Make notes of these ideas and say which ones you think would make the best stories.

Writing

PCM
23

1 Make notes for the plot of your own story.

2 Write notes of ideas for the setting.

3 Write notes for two characters.

REMEMBER

Keep your eyes and ears open.

Write about what you know.

Really see it in your imagination.

Extended Writing

Use your notes to write the first draft of your story.

Michael Morpurgo – Looking at a Manuscript

Extract from the first draft of the manuscript for *The Butterfly Lion*.

Transcript of the manuscript

(Everyone can see the lion for miles around)

(You have to turn sharp left outside the village. It's not marked.)

Butterflies only live short lives. They flower and flutter for just a few glorious days/weeks and then die. That's (probably) why /so very few people have ever seen the Butterfly Lion. But I have. I saw him by accident/ blue and shimmering in the sun/ one warm June morning when I was young. I was (sent at the age of eight to a) ten, and /away at boarding school in (Dor) (Wiltshire)/ deepest Dorset./It was a diet of Latin and stew and rugby and detentions./ and marks and squeaky beds and rice pudding. I didn't much like it. But most of all I was away from home. I often thought of running away, but only once ever plucked up the courage to do it.

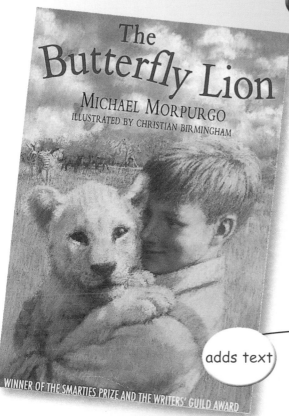

The Butterfly Lion

MICHAEL MORPURGO
ILLUSTRATED BY CHRISTIAN BIRMINGHAM

WINNER OF THE SMARTIES PRIZE AND THE WRITERS' GUILD AWARD

adds text

grips the reader

Chilblains and Semolina Pudding

Butterflies live only short lives. They flower and flutter for just a few glorious weeks, and then they die. To see them, you have to be in the right place, at the right time. And that's how it was when I saw the butterfly lion – I happened to be in just the right place, at just the right time. I didn't dream him. I didn't dream any of it. I saw him, blue and shimmering in the sun, one afternoon in June when I was young. A long time ago. But I don't forget. I mustn't forget. I promised them I wouldn't.

I was ten, and away at boarding school in deepest Wiltshire. I was far from home and I didn't want to be. It was a diet of Latin and stew and rugby and detentions and chilblains and marks and squeaky beds and semolina pudding. And then there was Basher Beaumont who terrorised and tormented me, so that I lived every waking moment of my life in dread of him. I had often thought of running away, but only ever once plucked up courage to do it.

Reading

1 Work with a partner on **sheet 24**.

   a On the final published version, highlight all the words and phrases which have been added since the transcript.

   b Discuss why you think Michael Morpurgo added them.

   c Do you think his changes make the story better?

2 Why do you think Michael Morpurgo decided to call the opening chapter '**Chilblains and Semolina Pudding**'?

Writing

1 Work with a partner. Read each other's story drafts from Unit 10.

2 Point out two things that work well.

3 Highlight two parts that could be improved.

4 Swap drafts and revise your work.

REMEMBER

clarity

detail

rhythm

Extended Writing

Write the final draft of your story. After writing two paragraphs, re-read and then edit for clarity and detail. Then write another two paragraphs.

NOTEMAKING

Then and Now

Notes on school and leisure in the 1930s and the present day

1930s

School

type
one sch 5 to 14
some go to grammar sch
40 chn in class

separates notes into categories →

age
start at 5
leave at 14 (work)

subjects
3 Rs
little space for PE
scholarship at 11yrs

Leisure

holidays
some week at sea
- Blackpool, Scarborough, Brighton
few go abroad
ships for passengers to America
- Qn Mary, Qn Elizabeth

games
games in street - not many cars
hoops, tops, yo-yos, marbles
clockwork trains

entertainment
listen wireless - chldren's hr
v. few TVs (b/w)
collect stamp and cig cards

NOW

School

type
primary sch 5-11
sec sch 11-16
college/6th form 16-18
5 day week

age
start at 5
leave at 16/some 18

subjects
Ma, Sc, Eng, Hi, Geog, PE,
DT, IT, Mu
computers

Leisure

holidays
hols abroad
- Spain, France, Caribbean
travel by plane

games
computer games
action figs
roller blading

entertainment
CDs
colour TVs
cinema
collect ftball stickers

SCHOOL IN THE 1930s

turns notes into sentences →

In the 1930s schools were very different from schools today. Children started school when they were five years old, and a lot of children left at the age of fourteen. Some went straight to work. Most children stayed at the same school, an elementary school, for the whole of their school life, from the age of 5 to 14. Most elementary schools were crowded and had little space for things like PE and games. Children spent most of their time learning the three 'Rs', – Reading, wRiting and aRithmetic. They sat down most of the time because there were usually about 40 children in each class.

Some children took a scholarship exam when they were 11, and if they passed, they could go on to a grammar school, where they could stay until they were 18.

By Rashid and Loretta

Reading

1. Work in pairs. Write these notes as sentences:

   a *primary sch 5–11*

   b *games in street – not many cars*

   c *v. few TVs (b/w)*

2. Complete the activity on **sheet 25**.

3. Plan two or three questions you might ask friends about their leisure interests and hobbies.

Writing

1. Work in pairs. One of you ask the questions that you planned in question 3 above. The other makes notes on the answers. Then swap tasks.

2. Look at your own notes. Underline notes about similar things.

3. Use your notes to draft a report on 'Children's Leisure Interests and Hobbies'. Divide your work into paragraphs.

REMEMBER

Write key points only.

Simplify words .

Write quickly.

Use abbreviations.

Extended Writing

Edit and rework your draft into a short report on 'Children's Leisure Interests and Hobbies'.

13

REVISE AND EDIT
Banana-Day Trip

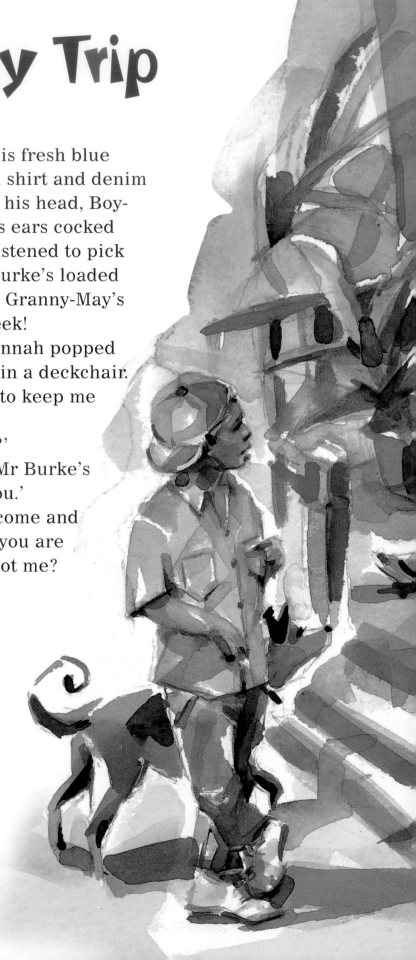

Dressed in his cleaned sneakers, his fresh blue denim trousers, denim short-sleeved shirt and denim long peaked cap turned sideways on his head, Boy-Don brushed his dog. But he kept his ears cocked
5 sharp. All the time he listened. He listened to pick out the distant horn-blowing of Mr Burke's loaded banana-truck that would take him to Granny-May's house. He'd stay there one whole week!

From nowhere, twelve-year-old Hannah popped
10 out on to the veranda. She sat down in a deckchair. Boy-Don said, 'My sister – you come to keep me company, or to trouble me?'

'Why you so impatient to get away?'

'I'm not on my way to Granny yet. Mr Burke's
15 taking ages getting me away from you.'

'Boy-Don, I was thinking. I had to come and talk to you. D'you know exactly why you are going to stay with Granny-May and not me? Or Andy? Or Mark?'
20 Boy-Don tossed his arms about. 'Jealous! Jealous! Jealous!'

'Favouritism! That's what it is. Favouritism!'

Boy-Don faced Hannah
25 crossly. 'Granny-May love me best. She love me best. Me is the one she love best.'

'Listen to him! Listen to him! Can't even talk properly.
30 If mamma could hear you.

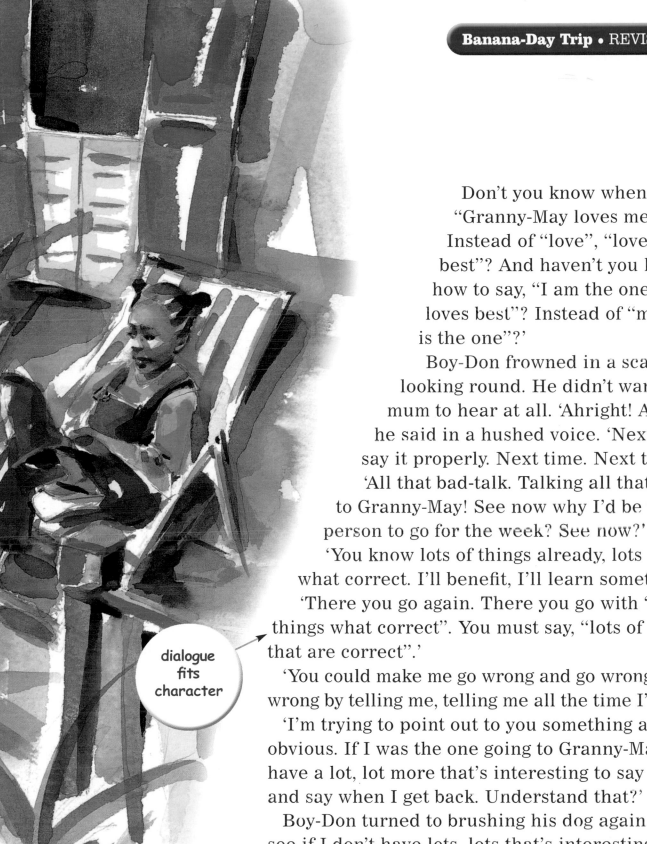

dialogue
fits
character

Don't you know when to say, "Granny-May loves me best"? Instead of "love", "loves me best"? And haven't you learnt yet how to say, "I am the one she loves best"? Instead of "me", "me is the one"?'　　35

Boy-Don frowned in a scared way, looking round. He didn't want their mum to hear at all. 'Ahright! Ahright!' he said in a hushed voice. 'Next time I say it properly. Next time. Next time.'　　40

'All that bad-talk. Talking all that bad-talk to Granny-May! See now why I'd be the fit person to go for the week? See now?'　　45

'You know lots of things already, lots of things what correct. I'll benefit, I'll learn something.'

'There you go again. There you go with "lots of things what correct". You must say, "lots of things that are correct".'　　50

'You could make me go wrong and go wrong and go wrong by telling me, telling me all the time I'm wrong.'

'I'm trying to point out to you something all obvious. If I was the one going to Granny-May I'd have a lot, lot more that's interesting to say there, and say when I get back. Understand that?'　　55

Boy-Don turned to brushing his dog again. 'You'll see if I don't have lots, lots that's interesting when I get back.'

*An extract from **The Future Telling Lady** by James Berry*

Reading

1 Do you think Hannah is jealous of her brother? Write down any clues from the text.

 2 Make a list of things about Boy-Don's life that are similar to your own, and those that are different.

3 Write a short paragraph comparing your experience of family life with Boy-Don's.

Writing

1 Work with a partner. Read each other's 'Family Life' story drafts.

2 Find two things you like and two things that could be improved.

3 Revise and edit the drafts together. Use the proof-reading marks shown on **sheet 27**.

REMEMBER

Use proof-reading marks.

Use your own experience.

Make the dialogue fit the characters.

Extended Writing

Continue to revise and edit your story, using the proof-reading marks. Write a clean, finished copy.

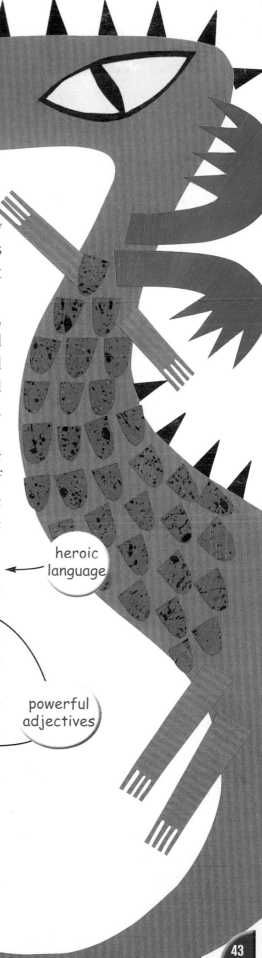

14

LEGENDS

Krakus and the Dragon

O N THE BANKS of the river Vistula there is a hill now known as the Wawel Hill. On that hill there stands today an ancient castle, and below lies the ancient city of Krakow, the former capital of Poland.

5   Long, long ago, there was no castle on the Wawel Hill, neither was there any city of Krakow, but only a few scattered villages where humble people lived who tilled the soil and minded their flocks. Poor though the people were, none could have been happier. They sang as they went about their work,
10 and their children's merry laughter echoed over the fields.

    But one day, happiness fled from the land. A dragon came down the river Vistula, a dragon that breathed forth flames of fire and shook the earth with its roars. It made its home inside a cave beneath the Wawel Hill, and the people
15 trembled with fear.

    'Have no fear,' the strongest men cried. 'The dragon shall not live!' Armed with axes fit to fell the mightiest trees, they went forth a hundred strong to slay the cruel monster.

heroic language

    As they neared the hill, the dragon left its cage and
20 plunged towards them, snorting flames and fiery fumes. The men, undaunted, rushed towards it, brandishing their axes, but all in vain. They could not reach the fiery monster; they could not use their mighty axes. Exhausted, scorched, and burning, they turned back in despair.

powerful adjectives

25   The people's fear was greater than before. They locked their children in their homes and drove away their flocks. No one was safe. The beast devoured every living thing it saw.

    At last, the people in their fear sought the help of one named Krakus, who was a wise and learned man.

30   'Help us, Krakus!' they cried. 'Of your wisdom tell us how we can destroy this dragon, before it destroys all of us!'

Krakus pondered the question long, rubbing his chin and wrinkling his brow. At last his eyes grew bright and he said, 'No man can slay this fire-breathing monster, but by a trick it shall be overcome.'

He bade the people return to their homes until he should bring them forth with a blast on his horn.

Then Krakus took a young lamb's skin and filled it up with tar and brimstone. In the darkness of the night he carried this to the Wawel Hill, and laid it before the dragon's cave while the beast was fast asleep and snoring. Then he crept away to the river's edge and hid among the bushes to await the dawn.

Krakus saw the dragon wake, pounce on the lamb and swallow it, and then writhe in agony. For the tar and brimstone went on fire inside the monster, and burned and tortured it. Groaning with pain and panting with thirst, the creature crawled to the river to drink. It drank and drank and drank, until it swelled so big that it could not move. But still it went on drinking; and at last it swelled so big it could swell no more. Then, with a bang louder than a thunder-clap, the dragon burst!

Krakus rejoiced. His trick had succeeded! He blew a note of triumph on his horn and the people flocked from their homes and gathered round him.

'Behold!' he cried. 'The dragon lives no more!'

The people cheered and cheered again. They hurled the beast into the river. 'We are free!' they shouted. 'Krakus has saved us! Krakus shall rule over us!'

Krakus answered, 'I shall serve you faithfully all my days, and may we always be free even as we are today!'

Retold by Lilian McCrea

dramatic climax

happy ending

Reading

1. Outline the story of **Krakus and the Dragon**. Work on **sheet 29**.

2. Find three sentences which describe the dragon. Copy them out and underline any powerful adjectives and verbs, using different colours.

3. Find two powerful adjectives used to describe Krakus. Write them down and add two more of your own.

Writing

1. Invent your own hero/heroine and monster.

2. Write one paragraph for your legend describing the monster when it first appears.

REMEMBER

Use powerful verbs and adjectives.

Use heroic language.

Exaggerate things.

Extended Writing

Plan and write the rest of your legend.

BALLADS

The Raggle Taggle Gypsies

Three gypsies stood at the castle gate,
They sang so high, they sang so low.
The lady sat in her chamber late.
Her heart it melted away as snow.

musical rhythm and rhyme

They sang so sweet, they sang so shrill,
That fast her tears began to flow.
And she laid down her silken gown,
Her golden rings and all her show.

She plucked off her high-heeled shoes,
A-made of Spanish leather, O.
She went out in the street, with her bare, bare, feet;
All out in the wind and weather, O.

uses
dialogue

'O saddle to me my milk-white steed,
And go and fetch my pony, O.
That I may ride and seek my bride,
Who is gone with the raggle taggle gypsies, O'.

O he rode high and he rode low.
He rode through wood and copses too.
Until he came to an open field,
And there he espied his lady, O'.

repeated
phrases

'What care I for my house and my land,
What care I for my treasure, O?
What care I for my new-wedded lord,
I'm off with the raggle taggle gypsies, O'.

'Last night you slept on a goose-feather bed,
With the sheets turned down so bravely, O.
And tonight you'll sleep in a cold open field,
Along with the raggle taggle gypsies, O'.

'What care I for a goose-feather bed,
With the sheets turned down so bravely, O?
For tonight I shall sleep in a cold open field
Along with the raggle taggle gypsies, O.'

sad story

Reading

❶ Work with a partner. One of you read the ballad again.

❷ The story '**The Raggle Taggle Gypsies**' is told in three short scenes, like a film. Draw three quick sketches on the storyboard (**sheet 31**) to show them.

❸ Choose a line from the ballad as a title for each scene. Write it beside each sketch.

Writing

PCM 33

❶ Work in pairs. Carry on revising the first draft of '**The Ballad of Old Lucy**'.

❷ Practise reading the revised ballad aloud, paying attention to the rhythm and mood.

REMEMBER

Ballad

story told through dialogue

regular rhythm and rhyme

repeated phrases

generally four lines in each verse

story conveyed through a few powerful scenes

Extended Writing

❶ Finish and polish your revisions.

❷ Write a new ballad of your own.

An Odd Kettle of Fish

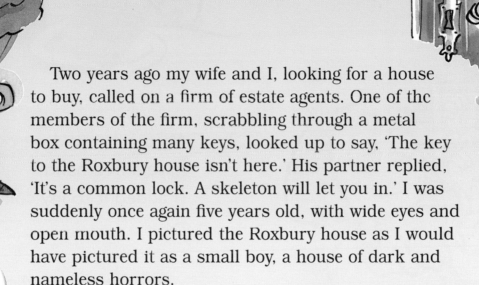

Two years ago my wife and I, looking for a house to buy, called on a firm of estate agents. One of the members of the firm, scrabbling through a metal box containing many keys, looked up to say, 'The key to the Roxbury house isn't here.' His partner replied, 'It's a common lock. A skeleton will let you in.' I was suddenly once again five years old, with wide eyes and open mouth. I pictured the Roxbury house as I would have pictured it as a small boy, a house of dark and nameless horrors.

figure of speech

Then there was the man who left town under a cloud. Sometimes I saw him all wrapped up in the cloud, and invisible, like a cat in a sack. At other times it floated, about the size of a sofa, three or four feet above his head, following him wherever he went.

literal meaning

There were many other wonderful figures: the old lady who was always up in the air, the man who lost his head during a fire but was still able to run out of the house yelling.

James Thurber

An Odd Kettle of Fish

1   The detectives said that
The books had been cooked.
(They tasted good.)

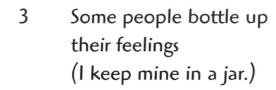

2   My teacher said we could
have a free hand.
(I added it to my collection.)

3   Some people bottle up
their feelings
(I keep mine in a jar.)

4   My mother said –
'Hold your tongue!'
(It was too slippery.)

5   When my sister laughs
she drives me round the bend.
(I catch the bus back.)

6   Dad told me
to keep a stiff upper lip.
(It's in a box by my bed.)

7   My Uncle is a terrible
name-dropper.
(I help my Aunt to sweep them up.)

8   In the school races
I licked everyone in the class.
(It made my tongue sore.)

Pie Corbett

Reading

PCM 34

1 Explain the **figurative** meaning of 'under a cloud'. Then draw an amusing picture to show its **literal** meaning.

2 Do the same for 'up in the air', 'skeleton key' and 'lost his head'.

3 Choose two more examples from the list of everday figures of speech, or think of two of your own. Explain their figurative and literal meanings. You could illustrate them.

Writing

PCM 36

1 Write a new verse for **'An Odd Kettle of Fish'**.

2 Choose an idiom from the class list. Who might say or do it? Write the first two lines.

3 Write the last line in brackets. It should say something about the **literal** meaning.

4 Draw a cartoon to illustrate the last line.

REMEMBER

The difference between figurative and literal.

Use the idioms list for ideas.

Use brackets for the last verse.

Extended Writing

Revise and edit your verses (you could write a few more) and produce in a final form with illustrations.

MYTHS
Lord Krishna's Flute

typical beginning

A long, long time ago, the god Vishnu came to Earth and became Lord Krishna. As a young man, Krishna loved to play the flute. He often went for walks in the forests and played for the animals there. They loved his beautiful music.

complex sentences

5 One day, after he had played for them, he fell asleep. He didn't know it but a young boy in ragged clothes had also been listening to his music. When he saw that Krishna was asleep, he crept up to Krishna's side and took the flute. He put it to his lips and tried to play it, but try as he might, he could not play a single tune. All he 10 could produce were odd, sharp notes which soon woke Krishna up.

The poor boy fell to his knees. 'Oh, my Lord Krishna,' he wept, 'I had no idea that you were a god. I did not steal your flute. I only wanted to try and play it as beautifully as you.'

Lord Krishna felt sorry for the boy, so he decided
15 to soften the punishment. 'Come, my boy,' he said,
and gently put his hands over the boy's mouth.
'From this time on, you will try to copy my song
but you will never succeed.' Then he touched the
boy's rags and whispered, 'You will also wear my
20 colours and stay in these forests forever.'

And with these words the boy turned into a
beautiful bird with the blue markings of Krishna
and began to sing the song of Krishna's flute. But
as Lord Krishna had foretold, it couldn't finish the
25 song. The bird became known as the Whistling
Thrush of Malabar. To this day, it is still trying to
finish the lovely song played by Krishna on his
magic flute.

RETOLD BY LINDA GANN

magical
happenings

why things
are as
they are

Reading

PCM 37

1 Write brief notes that explain what each paragraph is about.

2 What type of person do you think Lord Krishna is? Give examples of words or phrases from the text which tell you this.

Writing

Work in pairs. You are going to make up your own explanation of '**How the Magpies Raised the Sky**'.

1 Select one of the ideas from the flipchart or think of your own.

2 Plan a sequence of events, to tell the middle part of the story. Make notes on **sheet 39**.

3 Develop the first event. Write a few sentences.

REMEMBER

Use longer sentences – add detail.

Use adverbs to describe what the magpies did.

Use adjectives to describe the sky.

Use punctuation to help make the meaning clear.

Extended Writing

Carry on writing the middle section of '**How the Magpies Raised the Sky**'.

SOURCES

The Blue Whale

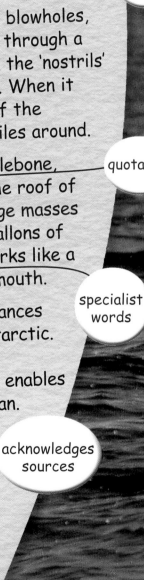

general opening

present tense

1 The blue whale is the largest creature on Earth and is found in all the world's oceans.

2 Blue whales can grow up to 29 metres long, (the length of six or more elephants). Their skin is light grey with a white mottled pattern.

3 On the highest point of a blue whale's head are two blowholes, like nostrils, through which it breathes. Air travels through a pipe leading to its huge lungs. When the whale dives, the 'nostrils' close and it can stay under water for up to an hour. When it re-surfaces, and breathes out, the air spurts out of the blowholes, causing a spray which can be seen for miles around.

quotation

4 The blue whale has no teeth, but has strips of whalebone, called baleen, that hang like a 'giant comb', from the roof of its mouth. When the whale feeds it lunges into large masses of sea creatures, such as krill, and thousands of gallons of water and food rush into its mouth. The baleen works like a sieve so that only the krill remains in the whale's mouth.

specialist words

5 Blue whales live in groups which migrate[1] huge distances between the tropics and the icy waters of the Antarctic. They make a series of moaning noises that reach 188 decibels[2], the loudest song of any animal. This enables them to communicate across vast expanses of ocean.

acknowledges sources

Bibliography
Grosvener, Donna K. The Blue Whale, National Geographic Society, 1977
O' Callahan, K. Staying Alive, Brimax, 1987
Platt, R. Wonders of Nature, Purnell, 1983
Wursig, Bernd G. Blue Whale, Microsoft Encarta, Encyclopaedia, 1997

1 Blue whales migrate to the edges of the ice pack to feed. They travel to the tropics to breed.

2 A sound that can only just be heard is one decibel. A whisper is 20 decibels.

Reading

1. Write down the key facts from paragraph 3.

2. Write down the key facts from paragraph 4.

3. Describe how the blue whale feeds, using your own words or a diagram.

Writing

1. Make a list of the things you want to know about the topic.

2. Use books or other sources, such as a CD-ROM, to find information. List the key facts only, under the heading *What I Learned*.

3. Make a note of the books you used, and arrange these as a bibliography.

REMEMBER

Use your own words.

Make a note of books used.

Create a bibliography.

Use footnotes to explain technical terms.

Extended Writing

Use your notes to prepare the first draft of a piece of writing about your area of research. Give it a heading.

From Ice to Water

Hayley

Melting ice

Location of ice	Prediction	Results	Explanation
Warm water	I think this one will melt second in 1 min 50 sec because I don't think warm water will get into the ice	This one actually came first in 3 min 46 secs	The ice melted fastest because the temperature around it was warm
Cold water	I think this one will melt last in 2 min 25 sec because the cold water will keep it cold	This one came second in 9 min 30 sec	The ice melted quickly because the cold water breaks through the ice
In air	I think this one will come first in 1 min 35 sec because the air is warm and an ice cube melts faster out of water	This one came in last in 24 min 22 sec!	The ice melted slowly because the air at room temperature doesn't get through as it does with the others

Melting ice

introduces
topic

Ice melts at different rates in warm water, cold water and in the air.

explains
step by
step

Ice melts fastest in warm water because the air all around it is warm. This causes all sides of the ice cube to break down.

Ice melts second fastest in cold water because the water causes the cube to crack. The water then breaks through the ice. This is

useful
connective

suprising because you might expect ice in <u>cold</u> water to take longest.

Ice left in the air takes longest to melt. This is because the air at room temperature doesn't get through to it as well as cold and warm water, probably because water is heavier than air and will press the ice more.

Hayley, aged 10

Reading

Look at Hayley's finished piece of writing on page 59.

1 Write the answers to the following questions. Remember to write them as explanations.

- Why did the sides of the cube in warm water break down?
- Why did the cube in cold water melt so quickly?
- Why did the cube in air take so long to melt?

2 Write a paragraph heading to explain what each paragraph is about.

Writing

PCM 43

Either:

1 Use your homework notes to write the first draft of your explanation.

OR

2 Continue the explanation begun in shared writing. Use the paragraph headings to help you.

REMEMBER

Use impersonal language.

What happened and why.

Use connectives.

Extended Writing

1 Finish your explanation. Proof-read each other's writing to check for spelling and punctuation. Make sure that each paragraph links with the one that goes before.

2 Draw and label a diagram to support your explanation.

Mountain Bikes

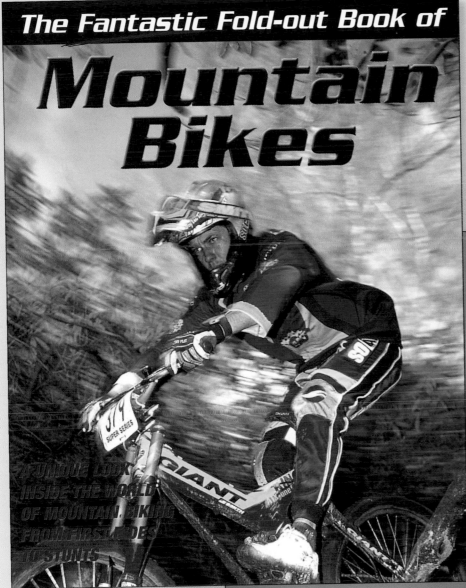

The Fantastic Fold-out Book of

Mountain Bikes

A UNIQUE LOOK INSIDE THE WORLD OF MOUNTAIN BIKING FROM FIRST RIDES TO STUNTS

introduces the topic

Contents

Learning to RIDE

When you have made your pre-ride checks, you can start pedalling. Find a flat area away from moving or parked cars, where you can practise operating the gears and brakes. Practise riding in circles, stopping quickly, and accelerating away from a standstill using your gears. When you are used to the way your bike works, or 'handles', you can ride in the real world.

SHIFTING GEARS

gives information

Mountain bikes have up to 24 gears. This allows you to pedal at the same rate, however steep the ground. The number of gears on your bike depends on how many chainrings and sprockets there are on a bike. A click of your left-hand gear lever moves the chainrings; the right-hand gear lever moves the sprockets.

explains how it works

PUT YOUR BRAKES ON!

Your mountain bike has very powerful front and rear brakes. They are operated by the brake levers on the handlebars. The left-hand lever operates the rear brake, and the right-hand lever operates the front brake. Take care – if you pull too hard on the front brake the bike may tip forwards. If you pull too hard on the rear brake the back wheel will skid. Try to balance the braking power of your brakes.

RULES ON THE ROAD

instructions use imperatives

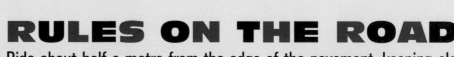

Ride about half a metre from the edge of the pavement, keeping clear of drains and gutters. Look ahead and take care, especially at junctions. Don't practise tricks or stunts – save those for safe areas away from cars.

TAKING CORNERS

Don't just turn the handlebars. Lean slightly towards the direction that you want to go. The faster you go, the more you need to lean.

PEDALLING

Keep the ball of your foot over the centre of the pedal. This will help you to keep better control of the bike.

GEAR TIPS *Avoid changing gear when you are pedalling hard.
*Unless you are racing or riding up a steep hill, ride in the middle chainring.

Reading

1 **a** What is the **main heading**?

b What are the **sub-headings**?

2 Write down **three things** that the book tells you how to do (instructions).

3 Find **one explanation**. Is it easy to follow? Explain why or why not.

Writing

PCM 44

PCM 45

Plan and write your own hobby booklet. You can work with a partner, but you will have to agree which hobby to write about.

1 Think of a catchy title for your booklet.

2 Decide what main headings you will need for each section.

3 Discuss what you will include in each section. Write down some sub-headings and sketch the layout for each page.

4 Make sure you include instructions and explanations.

REMEMBER

Hobby booklets

labelled diagrams or pictures

short commands for instructions

include explanations

numbering or bullet points

sub-headings

big print for main message

different fonts or lettering styles

some text in boxes

Extended Writing

Continue to work on your booklet. Swap first drafts with a partner and give feedback. Revise, edit and proof-read. Take time and care to produce a polished final version, good enough for the library.

Feathered Friends

Recount

PIGEON IN SCHOOL!

Neil Simpson brought a pigeon to school today for us all to look at. He held the pigeon upside down and opened the wing out to show us the wingspan. It was like a huge fan. I thought it was amazing!

The under-side of the pigeon's wing was white at the edge, but towards the middle, it became a darkish brown. At first, the neck was dark brown, but, when Neil held the pigeon in the sun it was a very shiny green colour. This shows that the neck is iridescent. The feet were a pinkie colour and the pigeon had three toes in front and one behind. It had a large wingspan, and the feathers got longer towards the edge of the wing.

Eleanor, age 9

Report

THE WOOD PIGEON

Wood pigeons are very common birds in the countryside and some can be seen in towns and parks, where they are quite tame. In woodland areas they are usually shy birds, and are difficult to watch, but are easier to see in open fields, and as they fly through the air.

includes facts, not opinions

The normal flight of the wood pigeon is fast and strong. Their wings make a clapping sound on take off and they use quick and regular wing beats and occasional glides, as they fly from tree to tree.

present tense

They make a five syllable cooing sound as they roost in trees, with the stress being on the second note. This sound can be heard all year round, but mainly in March and April, when they breed in woodland areas.

impersonal pronouns

The wood pigeon has a small head, short neck, stout body and short legs. It is bluish grey on top, with black markings on the wings, and a whitish rump. Underneath, it is purplish on the breast and bluish on the abdomen. The sides of the neck, especially in male pigeons, are iridescent.

Andrews, J. <u>Birds</u>, Hamlyn, 1978

gives sources

<u>Pigeon</u>, Microsoft Encarta, Encyclopaedia, 1997

Robert, age 10

Reading

1. Finish this sentence:

   Eleanor gives a personal opinion when she says, '.....................................'

2. **a** List the personal pronouns used by Eleanor in her first paragraph.

   b List three impersonal pronouns in Robert's first paragraph.

   PCM
   46

3. Look at Robert's writing. Write a heading for each paragraph which tells us what the content is.

Writing

PCM
48

As a group, you are going to write a short impersonal report, of no more than fifty words.

1. Decide which facts you want to include in your report. Group similar facts together using paragraph headings.

2. Write a short opening paragraph (one or two sentences) to introduce the topic.

3. Write the first draft of your report then read it through.

4. Count the words. If you have more than fifty, decide which to cut. If you have less than fifty words, decide where you might add more.

REMEMBER

Impersonal style

no personal pronouns

formal language

mainly present tense

no writer involvement

includes facts, not opinions

can include description

Extended Writing

Plan a short impersonal report about a person, place or thing you know well. Remember to use facts, not opinions. Write the report in the present tense. Use no more than 100 words. Include plenty of information.

If you use information from books, keep a note of which ones you use.

22

PERFORMANCE POETRY
Gran can you Rap?

Gran was in her chair she was taking a nap
When I tapped her on the shoulder to see if she could rap.
Gran can you rap? Can you rap? Can you gran?
And she opened one eye and said to me, Man,
5 I'm the best rapping Gran this world's ever seen
I'm a tip-top, slip-slap, rap-rap queen. ← catchy rhythm

And she rose from her chair in the corner of the room
And she started to rap with a bim-bam-boom, ← rhyme
And she rolled up her eyes and she rolled round her head
10 And as she rolled by this is what she said,
I'm the best rapping Gran this world's ever seen
I'm a nip-nap, yip-yap, rap-rap queen.

Then she rapped past my dad and she rapped past my mother,
She rapped past me and my little baby brother,
15 She rapped her arms narrow she rapped her arms wide,
She rapped through the door and she rapped outside,
I'm the best rapping Gran this world's ever seen
I'm a drip-drop, trip-trap, rap-rap queen.

She rapped down the garden she rapped down the street,
20 The neighbours all cheered and tapped their feet.
She rapped through the traffic lights as they turned red
As she rapped round the corner this is what she said,

chorus ➤ I'm the best rapping Gran this world's ever seen
I'm a flip-flap, hip-hop, rap-rap queen.

25 She rapped down the lane she rapped up the hill,
And as she disappeared she was rapping still.
I could hear Gran's voice saying, Listen man, ◄ everyday language
Listen to the rapping of the rap-rap Gran.
I'm the best rapping Gran this world's ever seen
30 I'm a –
    tip-top, slip-slap,
      nip-nap, yip-yap,
        hip-hop, trip-trap,
         touch yer cap,
        35 take a nap,
           happy, happy, happy, happy,
          rap-rap queen.

Jack Ousbey

Reading

1 How would you read the rap aloud together?

a Decide who will read which part.

b Decide which bits should be extra loud or quiet.

c Try reading the rap aloud. Adding claps and finger clicks or other sound effects.

d You could add some actions.

Writing

PCM 50

1 Work with a partner.
Write a new verse for '**Gran can you Rap?**'

2 Write your own rap.

a First, think of a catchy 'nonsense' chorus which tells the listener what your rap is about. For example:

> Give a clap slip slap
> For the Class 5 rap

b Write two pairs of lines that rhyme for each verse. For example:

> We're the best and we're in Class 5
> We're the best even dead or alive
> We ain't got brains, we ain't got cash,
> But we're all good-looking with plenty of dash.

REMEMBER

Use:
catchy rhythm
fast pace
rhymes
chorus
everyday language/slang

Extended Writing

Swap raps with a partner. Can you make them even better? Revise your own rap.

23

POINT OF VIEW

The Snargets

Barney has made friends with a caveman called Stig, who lives in a rubbish dump. Barney and Stig are hiding in their den. The Snarget brothers are thrashing around in the undergrowth nearby. They are looking for Barney …

'Cor, wait till I get my 'ands on you, mister Barney, wherever you are!' came the voice of the eldest Snarget. 'I'm all nettle stings one side of me face. We'll roll 'im in the nettles when we get 'im, that's
5 what we'll do.' He sounded as if he meant it, and Barney felt he was not quite so sorry for the Snargets.

The steps treading on dry twigs sounded quite close to the den. Barney moved further back into the cave and made signs to Stig to do the same, but Stig
10 stayed near the entrance. Suddenly the voice of the youngest Snarget piped up excitedly: 'There's a nole in 'ere, a nole! Come out of it!' And a large lump of chalk came flying in through the entrance and hit Stig smack on the side of the head.

15 Stig gave one roar and charged out of his doorway. Barney threw himself after him to see what would happen. The youngest Snarget gave one pop-eyed disbelieving look at
20 Stig and turned and fled, sobbing and screaming.

'Aaaaaaooooower! It's a kye – it's a kye – it's a kye – it's a kye – it's a K Y V E man!'

25 The other Snargets, who had been closing in when they heard the youngest's cry of discovery, saw Stig and turned and ran too.

'Wait for me! Wait, wait, don't leave me!' wailed the youngest, and then uttered a shrill scream of
30 terror as he put his foot through the bottom of a rusty enamel basin and fell headlong. 'ELP-ELP-ELP – 'e's-got-me-'e's-got-me-'e's-GOT-ME!!!'

Almost as alarmed as the young Snarget, Barney ran up to where Stig was standing over
35 the boy, who was shivering and moaning with fright and looked as if he expected to be eaten on the spot.

But Stig was standing there looking down at the fallen Snarget with an almost fatherly look in his eyes. He bent down to help the boy to his feet, and
40 the Snarget moaned feebly: 'Don't, don't.' Then, seeing Barney approaching, he turned his eyes pitifully towards Barney and wailed: 'don't let 'im 'urt me! Don't let 'im 'urt me! I wasn't doing no 'arm.' But Stig kept hold of him and led him firmly
45 but gently towards his den.

An extract from *Stig of the Dump* by Clive King

Writing

1. Imagine you are the youngest Snarget. See everything that happens through his eyes.

2. Plan and write an account of the incident. Use the paragraph outlines from shared writing and your notes from **sheet 51**.

3. Write two more paragraphs about the incident.

Reading

1. Think about what young Snarget would have been doing and thinking.

2. Make notes under the headings on **sheet 51**.

REMEMBER

Write as the youngest Snarget.

Use the first person – 'I...'.

Use the past tense.

Set out the dialogue correctly – as in extract.

Write to a paragraph plan.

Extended Writing

1. Add more paragraphs to show what might happen next.

2. Check and revise your work. Is it clear that the account is from the youngest Snarget's point of view? Ask a partner to proof-read your final version.

24

ARGUMENT

Leave Your Car at Home

Alternative Transport

Three pupils give their views on how to make transport more environmentally friendly.

Lee, age 9

The best way to get to school would be in a car that doesn't make pollution. I'd like a solar powered car but it wouldn't work because it isn't very sunny here. One man has made a car powered by water. He pours water in it and then does all the stuff to it to make it go. I'd prefer to get a water car over a normal one.

There's pollution because there are too many cars on the road. Buses are better because you can have 20 people on a bus but only one or two people travel in each car. Getting people to share cars is a good idea but some people don't want to share.

Using computers and the Internet instead of travelling to school or work is a good idea. I'd like to have my lessons at home with my teacher on a video recorder because if the teacher was being annoying I could switch her off.

Sarah, age 9

We should all have solar powered cars. They're really good – they don't have fumes like normal cars.

If we carry on using cars, cities will be hard to live in and the country won't be as nice as it is now. Sharing lifts to reduce the number of cars on the road doesn't work. If you wanted to go shopping, you wouldn't phone people up and ask them if they wanted to go too, would you?

The only way to stop people using the roads so much is to invent something that would fly but couldn't crash. It would have a laser out in front so it makes the craft able to dodge. You wouldn't be able to go to school with a laser craft or a jet pack because there'd be nowhere to land.

The best way to get to school would be in a car you had to pedal to generate electricity to make it run.

People should cycle everywhere. The Government should tell everyone not to use cars. They're useless, especially old ones. I only like sporty cars. I don't think you could use solar powered cars – you'd get stuck in them because when the sun wasn't out they wouldn't work.

Children should live near to their school. I walk to school because it's only round the corner. School buses are a really good idea too. The bus picks you up and takes you where you want.

In the future we should have space ships to travel in. But you couldn't go to school in a space ship or with a jet pack because there'd be nowhere to land.

I'd really like to see people use horses to get around.

Kim, age 8

Reading

1 Using **sheet 53** note down the arguments FOR and AGAINST the ideas for different ways of getting to school.

2 Which ideas do you like best? Choose your top three.

3 Think of three more ways of getting to school and write down the arguments for and against.

Note down the key words.

Use persuasive words and phrases.

Present your arguments FOR.

Shoot down arguments AGAINST.

Writing

PCM 55

Working with a partner, finish drafting the argument begun in shared writing.

If you wish you can write a different argument.

Extended Writing

Re-write your notes as a letter to the editor of a newspaper. If possible, send your letter to a local newspaper. Remember to use standard English in a formal letter.

25

NOVELS
Book Report

'You take it!' the chief was shouting, and he was shouting at me.

So I took up my father's oar and my share of the weight on my shoulder, and leaving Father behind on the dunes, we ran the gig down the beach and into the sea. We unlashed our oars, leapt in, and at once we were pulling hard for Samson. The waves hurled us up and down so violently that I thought the gig would break her back.

10 I just rowed and as I rowed I suddenly realised where I was, and what I was doing. I was out in the gig! I was rowing out to a wreck! I was doing what I had always most wanted to do all my life. At last, at last, at last!

15 And I rowed like I had never rowed before, fixing my eyes on the blade, pulling long and hard through the water, reaching far forward, bracing my feet and digging the oar again into the sea. The sea surged and churned around the gig. I became my oar, my oar
20 became me. I was too busy to feel any fear, too cold to feel any pain.

An extract from *The Wreck of the Zanzibar* by Michael Morpurgo

Reading

❶ Fill in thought bubbles for the characters in the story on **sheet 56**. Try to imagine what they are thinking and feeling. Write key words in the bubbles.

◆ Using **sheet 57** list some of the stories you have read recently. Whose point of view were they told from?

Writing

❶ Choose a book from your list. Make sure it's one you know really well.

❷ Write the first draft of a book report. Make sure you say enough about the plot but don't give away the whole story.

REMEMBER

Introduce with a summary.

Describe point(s) of view.

Describe effects of point of view.

Join clauses together with connectives.

Use connectives to link sentences.

Extended Writing

Compare two different characters from a novel.

26

EDITORIAL

Too Little, Too Late

No more half measures

Too little, too late. That's our view of the Government's plans to get more motorists out of their cars and onto public transport.

opening statement

reasons to support point of view

LOOK AT THE FACTS! A staggering ten million more cars are expected to be on the roads by 2025. Over three thousand people die on Britain's roads every year. One in seven children has asthma, triggered by traffic pollution. What's needed is a brave new approach.

Let's start with the school run. One in five cars in the morning rush hour is carrying a child to school. Trying to get people to share their cars simply doesn't work. So why not ban the use of cars for any journey to school of less than two miles? This certainly wouldn't be popular with everyone, but the benefits to children and the environment would be enormous.

A staggering ten million more cars are expected to be on the roads by 2025.

When children walk to school, they're starting the day with a healthy burst of exercise. Getting children out of the car, and into the fresh air is good for them.

— it's time to act!

Some children never see further than the inside of a car! How can we ask them to write a poem about a frosty morning or a walk in the rain?

Some schools have been setting an example by holding 'walk to school weeks', or organising 'virtual buses', where children are walked to school by parent volunteers, who pick up 'passengers', at different points along a route. This is the sort of direct action that can really make a difference.

One in seven children has asthma, triggered by traffic pollution.

So, let's see no more half measures. We must all start to show a real commitment to the environment, and the Government must lead the way. Only then will we begin to see how much better life can be, when the car is no longer king.

Jo Viner

point of view again in conclusion

Smog, caused by pollution, hovers above early morning traffic jams outside London.

Reading

1. Read the article and find one fact and one opinion.

2. Read each paragraph of the article to help you finish the sentences on **sheet 60**.

3. Using **sheet 61**, make notes about the content of the article and the writer's point of view.

Writing

1. Use the notes made in shared writing to write the first draft of an article for a local newspaper.

   You may want to write your own first and final paragraphs, or think of a different heading.

2. Edit and proof-read your first draft.

Extended Writing

1. Finish your article and make a neat copy.

2. Write another article on an issue of your choice – something you feel strongly about.

REMEMBER

Say what the issue is and give your point of view.

Give reasons to support your point of view.

Say point of view again in conclusion.

Style

use questions

appeal to the emotions

use short catchy sentences

use present tense

Agony Aunts

Letters to Wendy

I HATE MY MOLES

I'm really depressed and worried because I have loads of moles and big freckles all over my face and body.

Why has this happened to me and not to other people? Is there anything I can do to get rid of them? Please help me.

Miserable, Liverpool

Wendy says: Moles and freckles are often inherited and there's very little you can do about them.

Your freckles will fade slightly if you stay out of the sun (although you could miss out on a lot of fun) and you could have cosmetic surgery to remove the moles but it would be a radical step.

chatty, informal style

Your best bet is to accept that the moles and freckles are part of who you are and live with them. After all, millions of other people have them too.

HE COPIES ME

Every time I buy new clothes my mate buys the same thing. He's even had his hair cut in the same style as mine. He's a brilliant mate in every other way but this is starting to drive me mad. What can I do?

Donald, Northampton

Wendy says: It's understandable that this is getting to you, but don't let it jeopardise your friendship.

sympathises

Your mate obviously thinks you look good so you should feel flattered! Why not arrange to go into town with him one Saturday so you can help him find a style of his own? Happy shopping.

gives practical advice

I'VE GOT NO FRIENDS

I have no friends. Last year my best friend and I fell out. I really miss her because we had been best friends for years. My problem is that she now has lots of friends and is much more popular than me. To make matters worse, she's brainier than me and teachers are always praising her. We are in the same class and everyone would rather be friends with her than me. It's really getting me down.

Lonely, Newcastle

James Says

Friendships change and sadly some fade. It hurts to lose a mate you've known for years, but it's time to let go of the hurt and move on. Not everyone can be really popular at school, but everyone can find good, true friends and that counts a whole lot more, believe me. ← offers comfort

First of all try to be your own best friend – don't think about your imagined faults or compare yourself to others. Focus on your good points and make a real effort – smile, chat and be friendly to others and they'll respond in the same way. Try to find girls who share your interests and make time for everyone, not just the prettiest, most popular girls. If you're still unhappy after the summer, talk to your teacher to see if there's any chance of moving class. Making new mates takes time, but then so does anything worthwhile. Be patient – it'll happen.

Reading

1. Write about 'Lonely's' problem using **sheet 63**.

2. What are some of the most common problems for people of your age? Make a list.

3. Who would you talk or write to if you had a problem?

4. a Which Agony Aunt's answer do you think is most helpful? Why?

   b Which answer do you think is least helpful? Why?

Writing

Work with a partner.

a Compose a reply to one of the letters on **sheet 64**.

OR

b Continue the reply begun in shared writing.

> **REMEMBER**
>
> *chatty style*
> ....
> *keep it short*
> ....
> *sympathise*
> ....
> *comfort*
> ....
> *practical advice*

PCM 65

Extended Writing

1. Draft a new problem letter. The problem can be real or imaginary. Give the letter to a partner to respond to, or give it to your teacher if you prefer.

2. Reply to a problem letter composed during the lesson.

Child Labour

How is a rug made?

Has someone you know bought a rug recently? Does it show the 'Rugmark'?

In many countries, children are sold and made to work for a few pennies a week. Many of them make our carpets and rugs! It matters little to the bosses that the children work 16 hours a day, or that their hands are subject to premature arthritis. The Indian government, in response to public pressure, created a 'Rugmark', awarded only to those carpets and rugs that are made without child labour.

Next time that you or your family buy a rug or a carpet, look for the mark.

RUGMARK
International Trade Mark
015N182
293*187

Iqbal Masih

Iqbal Masih is a brave hero who spoke out against the cruel practice of forcing children into 'bonded labour'. Iqbal's parents sold him to a carpet factory when he was four. They were paid $12 for him – that's about £8! He was chained to a loom, beaten, and forced to work 12 hours a day. He never went to school.

Bonded labour

There are about 400 million working children around the world. Many of these children work in factories as 'slaves' under a system called **bonded labour**. The children's parents sell them to the factories because they can't afford to keep them.

The children earn a very low wage – about two pence a day. But they have to pay the factory more than this for their keep. This means that the children always owe the factory money, so they can never leave.

When he was ten, Iqbal escaped. He went to America and told people about the lives of the child slaves. In December 1994, Iqbal received a special Reebok prize for his brave heart and hard work – he said he was "no longer afraid" of the carpet manufacturer who had owned him.

Then, while he was cycling with two relatives in Pakistan, he was shot dead – probably by the carpet manufacturers who were worried about his campaign to free child slaves.

The publicity his story received has made sure that many kids like him in the world, who are kept behind locked doors, are never, ever going to be forgotten.

Reading

PCM 66

1. Read Iqbal's story again, then write a summary of it.

2. Finish this sentence:

   We should buy rugs with the *Rugmark* label because...

Writing

PCM 68

Work with a partner. Using your homework notes, compose a protest letter about child slavery in the football factory.

REMEMBER

Show your strong feelings.

Ask questions.

Get your facts right.

Argue clearly.

Take care to make it look good.

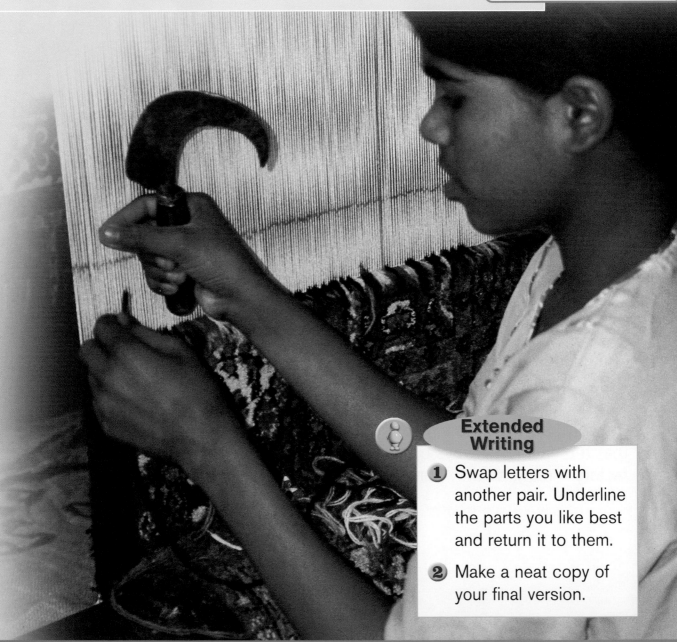

Extended Writing

1. Swap letters with another pair. Underline the parts you like best and return it to them.

2. Make a neat copy of your final version.

29 STORY ENDINGS
Hunt the Baby

Jacqueline Wilson

Who's there? Boo. Boo who? *No need to
cry, it's only a joke!* I'm Elsa. I'm always
telling jokes. I drive everyone daft.

I live in the Star Hotel. It's ever so posh.
5 Don't get the wrong idea. We're not rich.
We're so poor we lost our house and had to
live crowded into one room in a truly
crummy hotel, but then there was a fire
(I raised the alarm and got to be so famous I
10 was on television!) so for the moment we've
been re-housed. Well, re-hoteled.

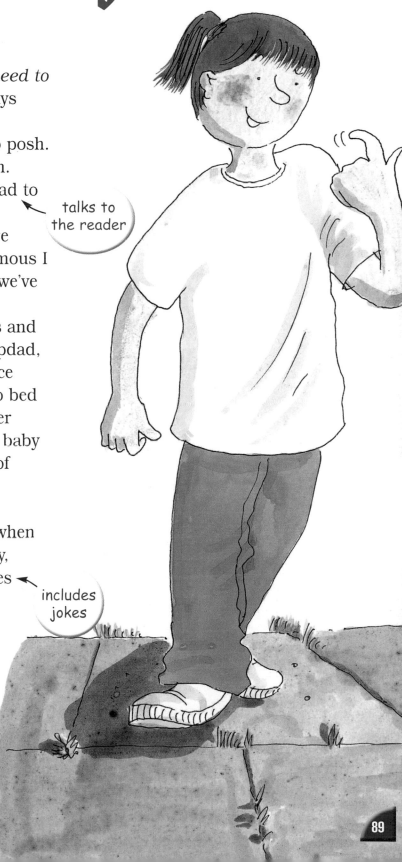

talks to
the reader

In the Star Hotel we feel like stars and
we all go twinkle-twinkle. Even my stepdad,
Mack. He hasn't smacked me once since
15 we've been here. My mum doesn't go to bed
during the day any more. My little sister
Pippa hasn't wet the bed once. But my baby
brother Hank hasn't half caused a lot of
trouble!

20 Hank doesn't cry much. He eats
heaps. He goes to sleep straight away when
you tuck him up in his bed. By the way,
what animal goes to sleep with its shoes
on? A *horse*! Hank goes to sleep in his
25 bed, yes. But he doesn't stay there.
Once he got right out the door and
down the corridor before we caught
up with him. He can't even walk
yet, but he's a champion crawler.

includes
jokes

30 He's never been properly lost
though – apart from the Sunday
we went to this car boot sale.

realistic language

It was a really super-duper sale, with ice-cream vans and sweet stalls and a roundabout for
35 little kids and heaps of people selling clothes and videos and T-shirts and toys. Mum spotted this fantastic sparkly top and started trying it on. She told me to watch Hank. Mack took Pippa off to get ice-creams. Aha – what did the baby ghost say
40 when he wanted his favourite food? I scream! I dashed after Mack to make sure mine had a chocolate flake and then I turned back to Hank in his buggy and ... you've guessed it. He'd slipped his reins and scarpered.

45 I searched everywhere. No Hank. Mum ran around calling him, stopping everyone to ask if they'd seen a baby boy. Nobody had. We started to panic. Mack and Pippa came back with the ice-creams and Mack got mega-miffed with me and I
50 thought maybe I was going to get smacked after all.

Reading

PCM 70

1 Look at **sheet 69**. Join the sentences with a connective to make one longer sentence.

2 What do you think the characters might say to each other when they realise Hank is missing? Write a page of dialogue. Remember the rules for writing dialogue.

REMEMBER

Include jokes, slang, realistic dialogue, tough characters.

Writing

1 Work out your own ending to the story. You can use ideas from shared writing or use your own ideas. Make brief notes.

2 Start to draft four or five paragraphs for the ending.

3 Swap endings with your partner. Give feedback to each other: something you like, and something which doesn't work so well.

4 Discuss ways of improving the ending. Try adding more dialogue, for instance, or more slang.

Extended Writing

Finish your first draft then revise and edit to make a final copy of your ending. Compare your ending with the original book if you can.

LEAFLET

NO SMOKING!

The following pages are from a leaflet to promote **No Smoking Day**. Your teacher will show you how the pages would be folded into a leaflet.

eye-catching cover

READY STEADY ST🚭P!

NO SMOKING DAY

MARCH 11TH

A leaflet to help you get ready to quit and give you tips on how to stay stopped

COVER

imperatives

NOW YOU'VE STOPPED

Stopping smoking for good is a big step, so remember:

- **Take one day at a time.** Congratulate yourself each day on your success.

- **Think positively.** If you're tempted to smoke, remind yourself why you have stopped.

- **Reward yourself.** Save the money you would have spent on cigarettes. It could be over £1000 a year! Treat yourself at the end of the first day, the first week, the first month.

- **Keep busy.** Do the garden, decorate, or take exercise.

- **Change your routine.** If you usually smoke when you're on the phone, have a cold drink handy instead.

- **Don't eat too much.** Stopping smoking can make you hungrier than usual. Avoid snacking on chocolate. Stick to raw vegetables and fruit.

- **Don't give in.** Don't think one cigarette won't hurt. It will. It will make you crave another.

- **Avoid temptation.** However well you are doing don't allow yourself to be tempted. If you want to talk to someone who understands, call the Smokers' Helpline. See back of this leaflet for details.

PAGE 4

GETTING READY – MAKE A PLAN

clear headings

Choose the day when you're going to stop. Think about when it will be easiest for you – midweek or at the weekend?

7 days before you stop

Check your reasons for stopping smoking against this list and make some of your own.

When I've stopped smoking I'll:

- reduce the risk of lung cancer
- be less likely to have a heart attack
- have more money
- be more likely to have a healthy baby
- set a good example to my children
- be fitter
- breathe more easily
- have fresher smelling breath, hair and clothes

My reasons

PAGE 2

6 days before

Try to understand your smoking habits. When do you smoke? Is your smoking linked to certain times of the day? Try to break these links. If you always smoke when you drink coffee, try drinking orange juice instead.

5 days to go

Tell your family and friends you've decided to stop. The more encouragement you get the more successful you will be, so ask for support and understanding. If you want some friendly advice call the Smokers' Helpline. See the back of this leaflet for details.

4 days before

Think about how you will keep your mind off cigarettes. Try to keep your hands and your mind busy. Now could be the time to take up a new hobby.

3 days to go

Stock up on nibbles – sugar free gum, raw vegetables or fruit.

2 days to go

Try to relax. Find out about exercise classes or look for books on relaxation and stress-reduction.

1 the day before

Now you're ready to stop smoking. Make sure there are no cigarettes around. Throw away your lighters and ashtrays.

PAGE 3

THE BENEFITS OF STOPPING FOR GOOD

- **Immediately** your body will begin to get rid of tobacco toxins.

- **After 8 hours** your blood will have half the levels of nicotine and carbon monoxide.

- **Within a few weeks** you will have a better sense of taste and smell, you will breathe more easily and your morning cough will get better. Your general health will improve and you will feel fitter.

- **Within a year or two** you will halve your risk of a heart attack.

- **After three years** your risk of a heart attack will be similar to that of a lifelong non-smoker.

- **After ten years** you will probably halve your risk of getting lung cancer.

bullet points

FURTHER HELP

For further help or information contact:

The Smokers' Helpline
For friendly help and advice on stopping smoking.

England Quitline®	0800 00 22 00
Scotland Smokeline	0800 84 84 84
Northern Ireland	01232 663281
Wales	0345 697 500

Your GP or health centre
Ask your doctor, practice nurse or health visitor for advice on stopping smoking.

Your local pharmacist
Your local pharmacist can give you advice and recommend a range of aids to help you stop smoking.

No Smoking Day
Unit 203
16 Baldwins Gardens
London EC1N 7RJ
No Smoking Day is a registered charity.

Reading

1 Scan page 5 of the leaflet – The benefits of stopping for good. Answer the questions on **sheet 71**.

2 Read the list of reasons for not smoking on page 2 of the leaflet. Choose the three reasons you think are the most important. Design a poster to persuade people to stop smoking, using the reasons you have chosen.

3 Make a list of the main headings in the leaflet. Write a sentence to explain what each part is about.

4 Do you think this leaflet is effective? Discuss it as a group and then either:

write down three things that you think make it work well,
OR
write down three reasons why you think it doesn't work.

Leaflets:

eye-catching cover

headings for each part

bullet points

numbering

use imperatives

Writing

1 Work with a partner. Draft the first half of a leaflet of your own, using the ideas from shared writing.

2 Design a cover for your leaflet. You will need a picture, a title, a date, and a summary of what the leaflet is for.

3 Draft the second and third pages, Getting Ready. Include a list of reasons why people should stop .... Then make some notes for the countdown from 3 to 1.

Extended Writing

Carry on working on your leaflet. Start to jot down a few ideas for the other sections, **Now You've Stopped**, and **The Benefits of Stopping for Good**.

Make a final version of the leaflet. Take time to lay out the lettering carefully. Include your names on the back cover.

Acknowledgements

TEXT

Unit 3: 'The Dark Streets of Kimball's Green', from *The Friday Miracle and Other Stories* © Joan Aiken Enterprises, 1969, extract used by permission of A M Heath & Co Ltd on behalf of Joan Aiken; **Unit 4**: 'Snake' © Keith Bosely, from *And I Dance*; **Unit 5**: from *The Angel of Nitshill Road* © Anne Fine, 1992, (Methuen Children's Books, an imprint of Egmont Children's Books Ltd); **Unit 6**: from *Working Children* by Wes Magee (Ginn); **Unit 8**: from *Vera Pratt and the Bishop's False Teeth* © Brough Girling, 1987 (Puffin, 1987); from *The Eighteenth Emergency* © Betsy Byars (Bodley Head, 1974); from *The Water Horse* by Dick King-Smith (Viking, 1990) © Fox Busters Ltd, 1990; **Unit 11**: from *The Butterfly Lion* © Michael Morpurgo (Collins Children's Books, 1996); **Unit 13**: from *The Future Telling Lady* © James Berry (Hamish Hamilton, 1991); **Unit 14**: from *Polish Folk Tales* retold by Lilian McCrea (Pitman and Sons, 1959); **Unit 16**: 'An Odd Kettle of Fish' © Pie Corbett, from *Crack Another Yolk* ed. John Foster (OUP, 1999); **Unit 17**: from *A Treasury of Asian Folk Tales* retold by Linda Gan; **Unit 20**: adapted from *Mountain Biking* by Brent Richards (A&C Black Ltd); **Unit 22**: 'Gran can you Rap?' © Jack Ousbey, from *Read Me: A Poem a Day* (Macmillan Children's Books, 1998); **Unit 23**: from *Stig of the Dump* © Clive King (Puffin Books, 1963); **Unit 25**: from *The Wreck of the Zanzibar* © Michael Morpurgo, 1995, (William Heinemann Ltd and Mammoth, an imprint of Egmont Children's Books Ltd); **Unit 26**: 'Leave Your Car at Home' © Children's Express, from *Learning Curve*, in *TES Primary Magazine*, Nov 1998; **Unit 28**: from *Stand up for your Rights*, ed. Peacechild International (Two-Can Publishing Ltd, 1998); **Unit 29**: from 'Hunt the Baby' by Jacqueline Wilson, in *Just What I Always Wanted* by Jacqueline Wilson et al, © Jacqueline Wilson (HarperCollins Publishers Ltd).

ILLUSTRATIONS

Unit 1: Chilham Castle, Kent News and Pictures Ltd; child picture © Penni Bickle; **Unit 2**: artwork by Gecko Ltd; pack shot by Yiorgos Nikiteas; book covers reproduced by permission of HarperCollins Publishers Ltd (*Collins Gem: Insects,* by Michael Chinery), Scholastic Ltd (*Cry of the Cat,* by R L Stine); **Unit 3**: artwork by Andrew Quelch; **Unit 4**: 'Witch's Cat' artwork by Nadine Faye-James; 'Snake' artwork by Tim Etheridge; **Unit 5**: artwork by Chris Molan; **Unit 6**: artwork by Alice Englander; **Unit 7**: artwork by Andrew Warrington; **Unit 8**: artwork for *Vera Pratt and the Bishop's False Teeth* by Chris Long; artwork for *The Eighteenth Emergency* by Abigail Conway; artwork for *The Water Horse* by Rosemary Woods; **Unit 9**: artwork by Jamie Sneddon; **Unit 10**: page 31, Penguin Children's Books; page 32, Michael Morpurgo; **Unit 12**: page 38, bottom left, Hulton Getty Picture Library; bottom right, © Mark Edwards, Still Pictures; page 39, bottom left, Hulton Getty Picture Library; top right, © Bojan Brecelj, Still Pictures; **Unit 13**: artwork by Karin Littlewood; **Unit 14**: artwork by Nadine Faye-James; **Unit 15**: artwork © Ruth Rivers; **Unit 16**: artwork for James Thurber extract by Clinton Banbury; artwork for 'An Odd Kettle of Fish' by Andrew Warrington; incidental artwork by Clinton Banbury; **Unit 17**: artwork by Kiran Ahmad; **Unit 18**: © Francois Gohier, Ardea; **Unit 19**: © Vincent Bretagnolle, Still Pictures; **Unit 20**: page 69 top right, © Peter Blake, Eye Ubiquitous; all other photos by Michael Rose; **Unit 21**: page 65 © G Verhaegan, Still Pictures; page 67, © Manfred Danegger, NHPA; children © Penni Bickle; **Unit 22**: artwork by Tim Kahane; **Unit 23**: artwork by Molly Swain; **Unit 24**: photos © Penni Bickle, with thanks to the staff and pupils of Summerhill Primary School, Hove; artwork by Clinton Banbury; **Unit 25**: artwork by Alice Englander; **Unit 26**: page 80, Amanda Gazidis, Environmental Images; page 81, © Mark Edwards, Still Pictures; page 82, © Hellier Mason, Still Pictures; **Unit 27**: photos © Penni Bickle; **Unit 28**: page 86, © Trip/H Rogers; rugmark © Joerg Boethling, Still Pictures; page 87, the Reebok Human Rights Foundation; page 88, © Trip/H Rogers; **Unit 29**: artwork by Nick Schon.

Every effort has been made to trace all copyright holders. The publisher would be glad to hear from any unacknowledged sources at the first opportunity.